MW01268900

CONTEMPORARY LIVES

MACKLEMORE & RYAN LEWIS

GRAMMY-WINNING HIP-HOP DUO

CONTEMPORARY LIVES

MACKLEMORE & RYAN LEWIS

GRAMMY-WINNING HIP-HOP DUO

by Judy Dodge Cummings

Essential Library

An Imprint of Abdo Publishing | www.abdopublishing.com

www.abdopublishing.com

Published by Abdo Publishing, a division of ABDO, PO Box 398166,
Minneapolis, Minnesota 55439. Copyright © 2015 by Abdo Consulting
Group, Inc. International copyrights reserved in all countries. No part of this
book may be reproduced in any form without written permission from the
publisher. Essential Library™ is a trademark and logo of Abdo Publishing.

Printed in the United States of America, North Mankato, Minnesota
092014
012015

Cover Photo: Todd Williamson/Invision for MTV/AP Images
Interior Photos: Todd Williamson/Invision for MTV/AP Images, 3;
Richard Shotwell/Invision/AP Images, 6–7, 98; Frank Micelotta/Invision/AP
Images, 11, 46–47, 97 (top); Brad Barket/Invision/AP Images, 15, 61; Elaine
Thompson/AP Images, 16–17, 96; Everett Collection, 19; Barry Brecheisen/
Invision/AP Images, 23; Chris Pizzello/Invision/AP Images, 24–25; JINY/
Splash News/Corbis, 27, 99 (bottom); Phil McCarten/Reuters/Corbis, 33;
Ted S. Warren/AP Images, 34–35; Brandon Wu/Retna Ltd./Corbis, 38;
Carlo Allegri/Invision/AP Images, 41, 100; John Shearer/Invision for MTV/
AP Images, 43, 99 (top); Jason Koerner/ZUMA Press/Corbis, 51; Robb D.
Cohen/Invision/AP Images, 55; Matt Sayles/Invision/AP Images, 56–57, 86,
89; Bruno Marzi/Splash News/Corbis, 64; Jordan Strauss/Invision for MTV/
AP Images, 68–69; John Davisson/Invision/AP Images, 72; Charles Sykes/
Invision/AP Images, 75, 77, 97 (bottom); Paul Buck/epa/Corbis, 81; Lisa
O'Connor/ZUMA Press/Corbis, 82–83; Danny Moloshok/Reuters/Corbis, 94

Editor: Melissa York
Series Designer: Emily Love

Library of Congress Control Number: 2014943854

Cataloging-in-Publication Data

Cummings, Judy Dodge.
 Macklemore & Ryan Lewis: Grammy-winning hip-hop duo / Judy Dodge
Cummings.
  p. cm. -- (Contemporary lives)
Includes bibliographical references and index.
ISBN 978-1-62403-545-6
1. Macklemore, 1983- --Juvenile literature. 2. Haggerty, Ben, 1983-
--Juvenile literature. 3. Lewis, Ryan, 1988- --Juvenile literature. 4.
Singers--United States--Biography--Juvenile literature. 5. Rap musicians-
-United States--Biography--Juvenile literature. 6. Hip-hop--United
States--Biography--Juvenile literature. 1. Title.
782.421649092--dc23
[B]
                                        2014943854

CONTENTS

1   **NOMINATED**   6

2   **RAISED ON RAP**   16

3   **A BOY FROM MIDDLE AMERICA**   24

4   **COLLEGE YEARS**   34

5   **MAKING *THE HEIST***   46

6   **GOING IT ALONE**   56

7   **FAME, FORTUNE, AND CONTROVERSY**   68

8   **GRAMMY NIGHT**   82

TIMELINE   96

GET THE SCOOP   100

GLOSSARY   102

ADDITIONAL RESOURCES   104

SOURCE NOTES   106

INDEX   110

ABOUT THE AUTHOR   112

Ben Haggerty, also known as Macklemore, *right*, and Ryan Lewis were thrilled at being nominated for their first Grammy Awards in 2013.

CHAPTER 1

Nominated

A t 7:00 p.m. on December 6, 2013, the Grammy Nominations Concert was scheduled to broadcast live from the Nokia Theatre in Los Angeles, California. Across the nation, pop, rap, rock, country, and classical fans sat before their televisions. However, 15 minutes before the show was to air, half the seats in the theater remained empty and people clogged the hallway and aisles. The announcer frantically urged latecomers to locate their seats. In minutes, the opening act would enter down the main aisle.

That first act was supposed to be rap artist Drake. However, just hours before the show was scheduled to air, Drake canceled his appearance. But the audience did not need to worry. Another group stepped in to take Drake's place.

The clock struck seven. Stragglers scrambled to find a seat as the host, rapper LL Cool J, took the stage. Dressed in a gray vest and black jacket and wearing a black beret, LL Cool J proclaimed, "Great songs make the world go round."[1] Then he kicked off the 2014 Grammy nominations by announcing the titles competing for Song of the Year. The artists included veterans and newbies: Pink, Bruno Mars, Katy Perry, Lorde, and Macklemore & Ryan Lewis. As LL Cool J announced each name, a snippet of the nominated song played in the background. The winning track would be announced at the Grammy Awards ceremony on January 26, 2014.

The applause was polite, but what the crowd really wanted was to hear some music. LL Cool J shouted into his microphone, "Are you ready?"[2] The audience roared back. Then the doors to the

Artists submit songs to be considered for Grammys in a particular musical genre. However, a subcommittee decides whether a song belongs in that category. For example, if an artist submits a song in the country category, the country subcommittee might decide the song is actually a rock 'n' roll song and eliminate it from consideration for a country Grammy. But the subcommittee does not have the final say. A general committee made up of representatives of other genres reviews the final nominations from all subcommittees. They can vote to override the subcommittee's decision.

Although Haggerty and Lewis define themselves as rappers, they were almost denied the chance to compete for a rap Grammy. After two of their songs hit Number 1 on the *Billboard* Hot 100 list last year, the rap subcommittee argued that since the pair's music had so much success on mainstream radio, they were actually a pop group. However, when the general committee listened to Macklemore & Ryan Lewis's album *The Heist*, they determined it was definitely in the rap music category.

hallway opened and the first act of the evening entered: Macklemore & Ryan Lewis.

This rap duo did not perform the song that had just earned them a Grammy nomination for Song of the Year. Instead, they sang the rafter-rocking, hand-clapping, foot-stomping number that had catapulted to the top of the charts in 2013: "Thrift Shop."

Ben Haggerty—known by the stage name Macklemore—strutted down the aisle. He sported a brown jacket with a wide fur collar. Clunky gold chains adorned his neck. Ryan Lewis followed. In contrast to Haggerty's over-the-top outfit, Lewis's classy red suit resembled a business executive more than a rapper. Fifty-one-year-old Seattle singer Michael Wansley, known as Wanz, came next. He wore a flashy peach jacket over a royal blue shirt, and sunglasses hid his eyes. Kenyan-born trumpeter Owuor Arunga brought up the rear, instrument in hand.

As the foursome moved toward the stage, Haggerty leaped in the air several times as if he could barely contain his excitement. People in the audience thrust shirts and scarves into his hands. Haggerty waved them in the air and flung them into the crowd. Lewis wielded his microphone like a baton, working the crowd into a frenzy of excitement. In a rumbling baritone, Wanz belted out the hook line: "I'm gonna pop some tags. Only got twenty dollars in my pocket."[3]

The duo's dynamic performance had the audience on its feet at the Grammy Awards Nominations concert in December 2013.

On stage, two racks of brightly colored shirts and dresses gave the set the flavor of a secondhand store. Lewis positioned himself at the highest point of the stage and manned the DJ equipment. Wanz danced and sang off to Haggerty's side, three female dancers dressed in black-and-white striped shirts gyrated around the stage. Arunga's trumpet was accompanied by a large brass and drum band. The audience was on its feet throughout the performance, singing along.

The performance of Macklemore & Ryan Lewis was a dynamic way to kick off the nominations

Hip-hop originated in the 1970s as a form of cultural and musical expression that included four key elements: break dance, graffiti art, DJs, and MCs. While the genre has changed over the last 40 years, DJs and MCs are still key parts of hip-hop music. Today, many people refer to rap and hip-hop interchangeably.

concert. Most people had predicted the hip-hop duo would receive at least one Grammy nomination. But hardly anyone, especially Haggerty and Lewis, was prepared for what the night would bring.

|||||||||||||||||||||||||||||||||||||||||||||||||||||||

WE NEVER EXPECTED THIS

The Grammy Nominations Concert was an hour packed with announcements and performances. Taylor Swift sang and danced via telecast from Sydney, Australia. Keith Urban and Miguel performed a duet. Lorde, the 17-year-old singer from New Zealand, crooned live. Throughout these numbers, Haggerty and Lewis sat in the front row of the theater, accompanied by Haggerty's fiancée and Lewis's girlfriend. As the hour sped by, their names were nominated in one category after another. The men grinned and shook their heads in disbelief. By the end of the night, they had garnered a grand total of seven Grammy nominations.

After the ceremony ended, the rap duo was interviewed backstage. One reporter asked what their first reaction was upon hearing they had been nominated for seven honors. Both men looked surprised, as though they had been too overwhelmed during the ceremony to tally up their total. Haggerty gestured at the reporter.

MUSIC UNLEASHES US

On January 7, 2014, two men boarded a New York City bus, one wearing a hoodie, the other carrying a boom box. Street performers are common in the Big Apple, and the riders ignored this pair. Seconds later, the boom box exploded in music. The man wearing the hoodie yanked it off and began rapping the song "Can't Hold Us." It was Haggerty. Lewis was behind him, tossing paper towels to the riders to wave like streamers. This surprise mini-concert was part of the run-up to the Grammy Awards on January 26, 2014. The promotional program called Music Unleashes Us was meant to connect the musicians and their music directly to the fans. By the end of the performance, most of the riders were on their feet, chanting and clapping. Even the bus driver joined in. Then the duo quietly exited the bus.

"Very surreal. It has not sunk in yet. I just found out that we had seven."[4] Lewis added it was "mind-blowing."[5]

The duo looked tired as they made their rounds among the journalists. Lewis described how they had rehearsed in the empty Nokia Theatre and how much more fun it was to perform before a huge and excited crowd. Then a reporter asked how it had felt to have received so much love from the fans over the last year. Haggerty replied that the goal of every songwriter was to connect with his fans. He was pleased their music resonated with people and the popularity they were experiencing was "beyond anything that we could have expected."[6]

Haggerty's astonishment is understandable. While the rap artist has been performing for most of his life, never before was he a national phenomenon. Still, perhaps no one should have been surprised Macklemore & Ryan Lewis received seven Grammy nominations. Music has been a focus of each of the duo's members since childhood, and their ingenuity and drive is what brought them to the brink of stardom.

As Macklemore & Ryan Lewis's fame continues growing, the world is coming to know their funky and fun style.

Haggerty was regionally popular in Seattle and Washington before he became famous nationwide.

CHAPTER 2

Raised on Rap

Ben Haggerty—known on stage as Macklemore—was born in Seattle, Washington, on June 19, 1983. His neighbor listened to hip-hop music, so Ben was introduced to the style when he was only in first grade. One of his earliest musical memories was listening to "The Humpty Dance" by Digital Underground, which came out in 1990. Ben copied the tape from his older friend and "became obsessed."[1]

Ben grew up in the pleasant Capitol Hill neighborhood of Seattle. In a song he wrote in 2005 called "Claiming the City," he described his average middle-class youth. "I grew up on Capitol Hill / With two parents and two cars. . . . We even had a swing set in our yard."[2] His father, Bill Haggerty, was the coowner of a successful office furniture company in Seattle, and his mother, Julie Schott, was a social worker.

Although his parents were not musical, they did encourage Ben and his two siblings to be creative. For Ben, that creativity emerged with a dramatic flair. He describes himself as a "weirdo kid."[3] He would wear underwear on the outside of his clothes and put on dance performances for friends

"THE HUMPTY DANCE"

In the summer of 1990, when Ben was only seven, "The Humpty Dance" hit the radio. The song was on the album *Sex Packets*, recorded by Digital Underground. The star of the song was rapper Shock-G who donned a fake nose and glasses and became Humpty Hump, a one-man show. The lyrics of "The Humpty Dance" were silly. And they were raunchy. But the deep, steady bass was absolutely danceable and fun. This song consumed the airwaves in the summer of 1990 and converted a young Ben into a lifelong lover of hip-hop.

Digital Underground was one of Ben's early music influences.

and family. When he was seven, his parents took him to see a performance of the Broadway musical *Cats*. Ben admits he dressed like a cat for the rest of the year.

His first try at MC'ing was in a fourth-grade talent show when he and a couple of friends rapped "Cool Like That" by the Digable Planets. They practiced for hours to perfect the show. Rap continued to be Ben's passion as he moved into middle school, along with skateboarding, but he admits these early raps "were just horrible."[4]

In his 20s, Haggerty developed a tool to deal with his addictive desires: Vipassana. This Buddhist meditation requires focused concentration. The person meditating must examine all of his or her actions, feelings, thoughts, and emotions. The goal is to understand the source of pain and desire and to release it. Haggerty practices meditation every morning. In 2009, he and Lewis released a song titled "Vipassana." The lyrics describe Haggerty's mediation process: "Yesterday? / Forget it / Tomorrow is? / Nada / The present is right here, through the breath, watch it."[5]

Haggerty has been sober since 2008, but he still goes on binges. However, instead of alcohol or marijuana, sugar is his go-to drug. Haggerty admits sometimes he'll go to a convenience store and spend $20 on candy and then pig out on it in his hotel room.

Ben developed a darker passion at a young age as well—alcohol. He took his first drink when he was 14. It was approximately 3:30 p.m. on a school day the first time he ever drank. He put on a song by the rapper Tupac and opened his parents' liquor cabinet. Then he drank a shot of booze and then another. Twelve shots later, Ben was very drunk and had fallen into an abyss that would take him years to climb out of.

HIGH SCHOOL

When Ben entered Garfield High School, he began using marijuana. Often during his freshman year he would show up for school early and find a couple of friends willing to pool their money together to buy some drugs and skip school.

Ben's parents withdrew him from Garfield and sent him to Nathan Hale High, a predominately white, wealthy school. The transfer did not stop his alcohol and drug use, but it did lead Ben deeper into music. He formed a rap group called Elevated Elements with four other students. He had long listened to the music of Tupac, Notorious B.I.G., and Wu-Tang Clan, all of whom were mainstream rappers. But during high school, Ben's tastes expanded. He became attracted to more funky, jazzy work by underground rappers such as Hieroglyphics, Freestyle Fellowship, and Del the Funky Homosapien.

In 2000, Ben spent the summer in New York City at the School of Visual Arts. Ben shopped at thrift shops and dressed in bell-bottoms, plaid, or the kind of clothes a grandfather might wear on the golf course. Then he would go out on the town in these outfits and assume a different persona. The flashy, eccentric character Ben pretended to be was someone he had invented for a class project—Professor Macklemore.

That same year Ben released his first extended play (EP) under the name Professor Macklemore. It was titled *Open Your Eyes* and contained five songs. Some aspects of this EP hint at the kind of musician Ben would grow up to be. The song "Welcome to the Culture" is an example

EARLY HIP-HOP HISTORY

In 1973 in New York's South Bronx neighborhood, Kool DJ Herc was DJing at a dance. He wanted to lengthen the drum break in a song, so Kool played the drum solo back-to-back with two records on two turntables. Other DJs imitated this technique. Eventually MCs, or masters of ceremonies, began introducing DJs and their songs. Over time these "rappers" started speaking in rhyme to the beats of the song.

In the 1980s, hip-hop music evolved. Each rapper had a distinct sound that reflected the rapper's region and community. Groups including Public Enemy made music with a political message. Salt-n-Pepa performed dance music. Rappers including LL Cool J and Run-DMC wowed crowds with their verbal skills. Also in the 1980s, artists created a radical new way of making music by sampling recordings of other artists and mixing them into a new composition.

Haggerty's Professor Macklemore character still influences his style.

of how, even as a 16-year-old, Ben could create complicated rhymes and showed he was not afraid to express his opinion through his lyrics. "Mentally we're manipulated by the music industry / It's conference, chivalry, creativity, lyrically, / Step up and take a stand."[6] Ben eventually dropped "Professor" from his stage name, but as Macklemore, he was evolving into a hip-hop artist destined to get attention.

Lewis's family taught him to be caring and charitable.

CHAPTER 3

A Boy from Middle America

S imilar to Haggerty, Ryan Lewis grew up in a comfortable middle-class family. Ryan was born on March 25, 1988, and grew up in Spokane, Washington, a city of 200,000 people close to the Canadian border.

Scott and Julie Lewis, Ryan's parents, both worked with nonprofit businesses, and their Christian religion was central to their family. Ryan's father was the regional director for the Christian youth organization Young Life. The Lewis family, including Ryan and his two older sisters, spent 13 summers at the organization's summer camp in British Columbia, Canada. Charity and empathy were instilled in Ryan at a young age. He worked on community service projects with his family and helped build orphanages and teach music to kids whose parents were in jail.

Ryan was also shaped by a family secret. Julie, Ryan's mother, is HIV-positive. In 1984, she gave birth to Ryan's oldest sister, Teresa. The birth was complicated, and Julie required a blood transfusion. This was before blood donations could be tested for the HIV virus. Years passed, and eventually she began feeling ill. Julie was finally diagnosed six and a half years after she contracted the virus. She was only 32 years old and had three small children by that time, the youngest being Ryan. Doctors gave her only a couple of years to live.

When Ryan was six years old, his parents told him and his sisters about his mother's disease.

Ryan got a tattoo of a red ribbon, the symbol for HIV/AIDS, in support of his mother.

Because there was such a stigma about HIV and AIDS at that time, the family wanted to keep her illness a secret from the community. But Ryan could not keep silent. Julie recalled Ryan told everyone she was sick, including his entire second-grade class and the woman who bagged groceries at the checkout line in their supermarket.

The mission of the 30/30 Project, initiated by Ryan Lewis and his family on April 22, 2014, is to build medical centers in poor countries. The first center will be built in a village in the African country of Malawi, where one in ten adults has AIDS. Currently, people in this village must drive two hours to reach a clinic. Lewis and Haggerty are the first donors to the 30/30 Project. Lewis is grateful his fame has allowed him to do this kind of work. "It's pretty amazing for me that my family could have this story, my mom could go through all of this and it could come to this point that I could use sort of the platform that's been provided to invest my time and energy into something that is just really positive."[2]

Once the ice was broken, however, Julie changed her mind. "It was kind of comic relief for our family because you didn't know when Ryan was going to bring it up or what he was going to say. I liked it because he kind of broke the stigma a little bit."[1]

Ryan believes that while his mother's HIV status made life difficult while he was growing up, it also broadened his mind. His mother became involved with the Spokane HIV/AIDS Speakers Bureau. Most of the other speakers in this bureau became close family friends, and now most of them are dead.

This impacted young Ryan. He knows how lucky his family is. "I didn't get it, my sisters didn't get it, my dad didn't get it. It could've been a totally different thing. I could not be here. And she could not be here. But she is."[3] Indeed, his mother is a 30-year HIV survivor. Ryan and his mother have recently partnered to celebrate her 30 years of survival with a charity project called 30/30.

||||||||||||||||||||||||||||||||||||||||||||||||||||||||||||

MAKING MUSIC

No one in Ryan's entire extended family plays a musical instrument. However, his parents bought him a guitar when he was only six years old. When he was ten, he became obsessed with it, playing for hours at a stretch.

> "Ryan was either asleep or going hard at whatever he was into. . . . He wanted to be in the next phase of life 'now' and not have to wait for it to come."[4]
>
> —SCOTT LEWIS

Throughout childhood, Ryan skipped from one musical genre to another. In elementary school,

Artists such as Ice-T, Snoop Dogg, and Schooly D led the emergence of a subgenre known as gangsta rap in the early 1990s. Rappers reported on life in the ghetto as they narrated stories about crime and the hard life of the big city. A feud between East Coast and West Coast rappers led to the still unsolved murders of rappers Tupac and Notorious B.I.G. By the late 1990s, hip-hop had become the most popular genre of music in the United States.

he and his best friend, Ryan Sanson, went through a hip-hop phase. They went to school wearing FUBU apparel and listened to rappers Snoop Dogg and Tupac.

Then Ryan entered junior high school and became a rocker. At age 13, he got some friends together and started a rock band called One Example. Ryan wrote the songs, played bass, and sang, but he soon realized he was not a good enough singer. They performed in local competitions and at youth centers. Ryan began dabbling in the business side of music. He designed the band's T-shirts and website and promoted them. Ryan's bandmates eventually kicked him out of the band because they felt he took it too seriously.

At Ferris High School, Ryan stayed out of trouble, but he did not excel. He was more interested in skateboarding and music than academics. In 2004, he started a new band, Schema. This was during his heavy metal phase. He listened to bands such as Norma Jean, Underoath, and the Bled.

In the middle of his sophomore year, Ryan's parents moved the family from Spokane to Seattle, and Ryan's musical tastes transitioned again. He began listening to hip-hop bands such as Wu-Tang Clan and RJD2, and he began making beats of his

R-RATED

Although Ryan was a good kid who rarely got into trouble, there is one incident the family remembers well. The Lewis family children were not allowed to buy music CDs with explicit lyrics before they were high school age. When Ryan was 12, he bought three CDs with a parental advisory label on them. When his dad discovered them, he snapped the discs in half. Ryan's mother said the family laughs about the incident now. She said if a young Ryan had wanted to listen to "Thrift Shop," he would have had to purchase an edited version.

DJs rely on technology to create the distinct sound of hip-hop. The four main pieces of equipment that make up a DJ's toolbox are the turntable, synthesizer, drum machine, and sampler. Drums are the backbone of hip-hop music. These percussion sounds are repeated and layered over samples of sounds from already produced songs, and the DJ plays with tone and volume to create a texture to the music that will be the backdrop to the rapper's lyrics.

own. The switch from the jock-oriented Ferris High to the art-intensive Roosevelt High was a difficult transition. Ryan felt high school was a waste of time, and he wanted out. So he enrolled in summer classes, and in 2005 he graduated from high school one year early.

At this point in his life, Ryan decided beat making was not just a hobby. If he wanted his musical work to be taken seriously, it was time to get his name out there, "whether they [the beats] suck or not."[5] One man would take Ryan's beats very seriously. His name was Ben Haggerty.

Lewis might be less recognized than his flashy partner, but he is equally important to the duo's success.

Haggerty remains involved in youth outreach, filming an antibullying video with the Seattle Mariners baseball team in April 2014.

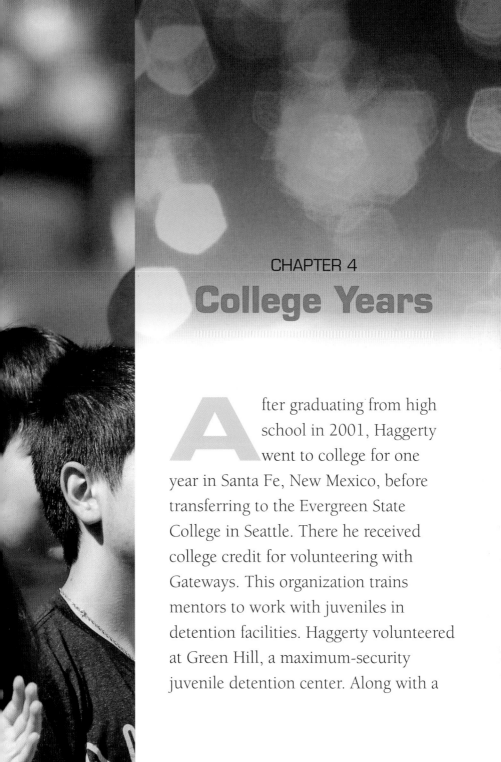

CHAPTER 4

College Years

After graduating from high school in 2001, Haggerty went to college for one year in Santa Fe, New Mexico, before transferring to the Evergreen State College in Seattle. There he received college credit for volunteering with Gateways. This organization trains mentors to work with juveniles in detention facilities. Haggerty volunteered at Green Hill, a maximum-security juvenile detention center. Along with a

The Gateways program Haggerty worked with is one of many programs that brings music into prisons. Since the early 1900s, music has been part of academic and recreation programs in correctional institutions across the country. Even maximum-security prisons allow inmates to take music lessons or even form prison bands. Music is used as a tool to help prisoners rebuild a positive identity. Many criminal justice experts argue that playing music together can help break down the racial and ethnic barriers between prisoners. Music also helps reduce tension and anxiety, and some studies show music programs help reduce the number of prisoners who commit crimes once they are released. One prisoner in Ohio's Marion Correctional Institution said he "traded a pistol for a trumpet."[2]

cofacilitator, he led writing workshops. Haggerty brought beats to the jail, and kids wrote their own rap lyrics. He helped organize a talent show where the teens performed for one another. Haggerty said working with these teens gave him a wider perspective on life. Although many people described these teens as the worst of the worst, Haggerty disagrees. He said, "They were great kids who got caught up in other things in their lives."[1]

MYSPACE

During college Haggerty kept making music. He recorded his first single, "Welcome to Myspace," in 2004. Myspace was one of the first social media sites, and it operated similarly to Facebook. Haggerty's lyrics were tongue-in-cheek, making fun of how easy it was to get obsessed with checking the status of your Myspace page. Haggerty e-mailed his song to Tom Anderson, the founder of Myspace, who in turn sent it off to his millions of Myspace friends. The next morning Haggerty opened his e-mail to find more than 10,000 messages.[3] The instant fame was hard to deal with. As the attention from fans grew, so did the pressure. Haggerty turned to drugs to escape.

At this time Haggerty was working with his friend Josh Karp, also known as Budo. As Haggerty slid deeper into drugs and alcohol, Budo was left with the work of producing the pair's album. Finally, in 2005 they released their debut album, *The Language of My World*, under the name Macklemore. It received a lot of praise and sold 7,000 copies.[4] Haggerty and Budo went on tour for a year, performing on the indie rap circuit. In 2006, they performed at Bumbershoot, a music

Today, Haggerty's early collaborator Budo produces for other rap groups, and he released his own second album in 2013.

and art festival in Seattle. When Haggerty saw the crowd of young people cheering, his ego started to swell. "I started looking at myself in a different way. . . . I started writing for the wrong reasons. I started looking for attention for the wrong reasons."[5] He forgot what it meant to be humble and became more concerned with fame than making good music.

After their tour ended, Haggerty and Budo tried to work on a second album, but Haggerty withdrew from family, friends, and music. He escalated from alcohol and marijuana to cough syrup and prescription painkillers. Haggerty realized he could not make music when he was high, so every few months he got sober long enough to write a few songs. Then he would start using again. It was during this troubled time in his life Haggerty first met Ryan Lewis.

THE PAIR MEETS

After graduating from Roosevelt High School a year ahead of his class, Lewis enrolled in North Seattle Community College. He learned to play the keyboard and experimented with music production software as he continued making beats.

Lewis also branched out into other interests. He worked for the school newspaper and learned graphic design and photography. Lewis eventually started his own photography business and found a niche taking pictures of local rappers. One day in 2006, he logged on to Myspace and friend-requested the rapper called Macklemore.

Lewis had composed a beat and posted it to Myspace. Haggerty liked it and asked if they could meet up and talk music. This was a life-changing moment for both men, although it would take a while before either of them realized it.

The first time the pair met in person, Haggerty was high. He pulled up to the Lewis home in his silver Honda Civic, wearing fuzzy purple sweatpants dotted with bleach stains. Lewis was not put off. Each man recognized in the other a hunger to make something of his music. Lewis showed Haggerty his beats, as well as some song samples and photographs. A couple of days later, they got together for a photo shoot.

FINDING LOVE ON MYSPACE

Haggerty did not meet only Lewis on Myspace. One day, Haggerty received a Myspace message from a fan, Tricia Davis. She had liked a song of his that she heard played on a Seattle radio station. The two went on a picnic and fell in love. This was during a four-month stint when Haggerty was sober. The next years were a challenge, as Haggerty slid back into addiction and cheated on Davis. But they stuck together and got engaged in January 2013. Davis is also the manager of Macklemore & Ryan Lewis.

Haggerty and Lewis's first meeting only hinted at how fruitful their collaboration would become.

The pair got along well, but it was not yet the right moment for their partnership to take off. Lewis was a busy college student with no plans for a career in music, and Haggerty was struggling with addiction.

|||||||||||||||||||||||||||||||||||||||||||||||||||||||

AN ARTLESS ADDICTION

Despite the early success of his debut album, Haggerty's career was slipping away. Any money he made he spent on sneakers and drugs. He reached for a marijuana cigarette before he even got out of bed in the morning. He missed family events and skipped shows he was supposed to perform in. Soon he stopped getting gigs. His partner Josh Karp moved on to producing music for other artists.

Haggerty hit bottom in the summer of 2007. He had experimented several times with the prescription painkiller OxyContin but decided to sober up for an upcoming family function. The withdrawal symptoms were torture. He would wake up at night and literally wring the sweat from his sheets. One day he left a frustrating recording session and sank to the ground, burying his head in his hands as tears washed down his cheeks. Years later Haggerty described that moment: "I couldn't remember what it was to be happy. I couldn't believe I'd let it get like that."[6]

Haggerty did stop taking prescription painkillers after this low moment, but he was still hooked on alcohol and other drugs. Finally, in 2008, his father persuaded him to go to rehab. This marked a turning point in Haggerty's life.

Haggerty's relationship with Tricia Davis, his fiancée, is another incentive keeping him sober today.

REHABILITATION

In rehab, Haggerty rediscovered spirituality and faith. His sponsor at the rehab center was a Buddhist. He invited Haggerty to come to his temple and try meditation as a tool for sobriety. During one mediation session, Haggerty had a realization. "People were chanting and doing mantras, it was beautiful. I remembered what it was like to be connected, to have a faith and connection to God, and know that it's bigger than me. I remembered everything that I had forgotten."[7]

When Haggerty emerged from rehab, he was clearheaded and hungry to make music. In 2009, he released *The Unplanned Mixtape*. This collection of five tracks included "The Town," a sort of love ballad to his hometown Seattle. Another tune on the mixtape was very different. The party dance song "And We Danced" has no serious or deep message. *The Unplanned Mixed Tape* was the beginning of Haggerty's comeback. Meanwhile, Lewis had also reached a turning point in his life.

|||||||||||||||||||||||||||||||||||||||||||||||||||||||||||||

WHAT NEXT?

At the University of Washington, Lewis was majoring in the comparative history of ideas. Lewis had many interests in addition to music, and this flexible major allowed him to create his own course of study. He combined history, philosophy, and comparative religion along with travel and photography. In a 2013 interview Lewis said, "I really liked that it was an open-ended major that allowed me to pursue my passions. It was a great fit for me and I miss it a lot."[8]

As Lewis neared graduation, the practical need for a job and a paycheck loomed. It was 2009, and the nation was in a recession. This was a bad time to find work in any field, especially with a college major like Lewis's. He figured he would have to take a job in graphic design or marketing. He never dreamed a music career could pay the bills.

FAKE EMPIRE

Lewis produced a short film titled *Fake Empire* for his college thesis. The film starts with the Disney logo, a Cinderella castle. Then the words *Fake Empire* spring onto the screen. The video shows a series of photographs of people with corporate logos taped over their mouths. Haggerty is shown waking up and checking his phone, then logging on to Facebook, and later moving through the day with his iPod in his ears. The film is a powerful depiction of how easily people are sucked into a consumer world that isolates them from real life.

Haggerty and Lewis agreed on an equal partnership from the start.

CHAPTER 5

Making
The Heist

Fresh from rehab in 2008,
Haggerty moved into his
parents' basement. He was
broke and took a job selling hats.
Lewis, only a few months from college
graduation, sent out dozens of job
resumes and did not get a single
interview. Then Haggerty and Lewis
reconnected. They decided to produce an
EP together.

This was the point when Macklemore became Macklemore & Ryan Lewis. Lewis told Haggerty he would not produce the EP unless his name was on it. He had heard stories of record producers and DJs who made good music but received no credit. He also knew most of Haggerty's earlier fame had vanished while he was struggling with his addictions. Lewis said,

> Both of us, on some level, were a little bit starting from square one. And I was going to do the photography, the graphic design, redesign our Myspace pages, make a website, mix a record, make all the beats, record all of the people, engineer it, track all of them. I was like, "This is about to be Macklemore and Ryan Lewis."[1]

Haggerty agreed.

IIIIIIIIIIIIIIIIIIIIIIIIIIIIIIIIIIIIIIIIIIIIIIIIIIIIIIIIIIIII

BUILDING A FAN BASE

The EP, titled *VS*, was released in 2009. One year later Haggerty and Lewis remixed the songs, added some new sounds, and reissued it as *VS. Redux*. A key single on the original *VS* and the *VS. Redux* is "Otherside," a haunting lament about Haggerty's

Music videos helped Macklemore & Ryan Lewis sell their songs. Some of the videos are wild and zany. "And We Danced" features Haggerty as Raven Bowie, a party animal who wears a gold leotard and a blond wig. Lewis explains, "Music videos are the catalyst for bringing the song to the next level. It's more entertaining."[2]

Others are somber. The music video for "Otherside" has a close-up of Haggerty's face as he lies in a bathtub struggling with the guilt and shame of his drug addiction. The song "Otherside" tells the story of Chad Butler, also known as Pimp C, a rapper who died from a combination of a sleep disorder and the abuse of codeine-laced cough medicine. The lyrics of "Otherside" reveal Haggerty's pain. "That rush, that drug, that dope. . . . Thinking I would never do that, not that drug . . . Swore I was going to be someone."[3]

struggles with drugs. The duo's fan base in Seattle grew. When they sold out three consecutive shows in 2011, they realized they might just be able to make a living from their music.

Haggerty quit his job selling hats, and Lewis held off on applying for more jobs. They rented a 500-square-foot (50 sq m) storage unit in a rough neighborhood as their studio. It was next door to a paint shop that blew toxic fumes in all day. They hardly had any money, but they did not give up. They were determined to produce a full-length album. This process would take three long years.

||||||||||||||||||||||||||||||||||||||||||||||||||||||||||||

COLLABORATING

The debut album of Macklemore & Ryan Lewis was a long, slow process for a couple of reasons. Lewis and Haggerty wanted to use live musicians instead of samples like they had used on *VS*. And collaboration takes time. Haggerty and Lewis worked closely, exchanging ideas back and forth. First the vocals were recorded and then the basic beats. Next the pair continued composing and rebuilding around the lyrics. Lewis described the process: "So it's an ongoing, back-and-forth thing. It could be a case of he wrote a verse to my beat, but once I got the verse I make all these changes within the beat that I think work better."[4]

Both Haggerty and Lewis are perfectionists. They are fortunate because their vision and styles complement each other, but these high standards were another reason *The Heist* took three years to make. In an interview in 2011, Lewis said perfectionism "makes for great art, but it also

THE HEIST

An intense collaborative
effort made *The Heist*'s
music and performances
the best they could be.

makes things take a very long time."[5] Haggerty said sometimes he was exhausted and just wanted to go home and sleep. However, he knew reaching the utmost potential of musical creativity requires sacrifice, and he said he and Lewis had sacrificed everything in the months leading up to the release of *The Heist*. Lewis agreed. He said that to maintain their level of creativity, it required a 70- to 80-hour workweek, working every single day.

"Massive things that happened for us this year were a matter of luck and the stars aligning. But we've been working . . . every day since 2009. . . . So there was a lot of steady, hard work and a real organic growth of our fan base, before the mainstream got access to us and radio airplay happened."[6]

—*RYAN LEWIS*

LEWIS IS NOT JUST A BEAT MAKER

The diverse talents and interests of Lewis helped fuel the success of the hip-hop duo. Lewis likes writing music, but he is equally interested in

The musical group Macklemore & Ryan Lewis is a four-person team with homegrown roots. In addition to Haggerty and Lewis, Zach Quillen is the group's manager, and Tricia Davis, Haggerty's fiancée, is their road manager and video producer. Unlike many celebrities who rely on stars to sing spots on their songs, Haggerty and Lewis hire Seattle acts. *The Heist* features the musical talents of locals Michael Wansley (Wanz), Ray Dalton, and Mary Lambert. Wanz was a rock singer turned software engineer. Dalton sang with a gospel group, and Lambert was a Seattle folk singer.

mixing it. He tries to develop textures in the sounds to support Haggerty's lyrics, and he sees himself as a sort of sculptor of sound.

Lewis always knew he wanted to do more than just make beats. He produces the songs, as well as directs and edits the music videos. He does much of the band's photography, graphic design, and web design. As the recording engineer, Lewis mans the control panel during recording sessions. He adjusts microphones and amplifiers to get a balanced sound. Each vocalist or instrumental track is recorded individually. After all recording is done, Lewis mixes the tracks to get the best final sound. He adjusts the volume of each track and

Macklemore is recognized on the street and mobbed by fans. But many people do not know who Lewis is. In an interview with *Rolling Stone*, Lewis said,

> I think on the mainstream level, nobody knows what . . . I am. Am I the DJ? Do I make the beats? Do I rap? Am I singing on tracks? . . . Why is that? Because the general public . . . based on my choice to be behind the camera as opposed to in front of it, are going to be more receptive to "Macklemore." The public don't care how the song came together. And I can't change that. So if I have jealousy, deriving from that, then that's just stupid.[7]

Haggerty gives credit where credit is due. "I wouldn't be in this position if it wasn't for him. . . . We're a team, and I'm extremely blessed because of it."[8]

adds special effects to the guitars or percussion sounds. Lewis claims he is not a control freak, but he believes that all the little things matter, even down to the style of font that spells out *The Heist* on their album cover.

DJing during performances is only a small part of Lewis's contributions to the duo.

The duo decided early on to rely on its fans rather than a record label.

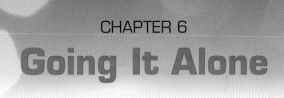

CHAPTER 6

Going It Alone

*T*he Heist was scheduled for release in October 2012. Along with their manager, Zach Quillen, Haggerty and Lewis developed a risky and revolutionary method to market their music.

In 2011, Quillen was working with the talent agency Agency Group booking tours for hip-hop artists when he attended a concert and saw Haggerty and Lewis playing the opening act. Quillen saw the screaming fans, including hordes

In 2010, as the Macklemore & Ryan Lewis tour van drove through California, Haggerty got the idea to start a fan club. He wanted their music to have a logo that represented their sound and the people who supported it. Haggerty has always been fascinated by sharks: "Great White Sharks in particular, but really all sharks. Tiger sharks, Hammer Heads. Dolphins."[1] He came up with the name Shark Face Gang and tweeted it. The next thing he knew, fans were coming to their concerts in homemade #SHARKFACEGANG T-shirts. Thus, the Macklemore & Ryan Lewis fan club was born.

of Macklemore & Ryan Lewis fan club members known as the Shark Face Gang, and was convinced the pair was going somewhere. He signed on as their manager.

The traditional way a band gets the money it needs to reach a national audience is to first develop a strong fan base. The major record labels, such as Sony or Universal, want to feel confident a band is worth backing. Once the artists sign a contract with the record label, the company promotes the group's music and gets their songs on the radio. However, in return the artists sign over a huge percentage of their profits to the record label.

Haggerty and Lewis did not want to forfeit any of their financial or creative control, so Quillen took a different approach.

He developed a three-step promotional strategy to use in advance of releasing *The Heist*. Macklemore & Ryan Lewis went on a 50-concert tour in the United States. These were small concerts, but they sold out and word spread, creating new fans. The group put music videos of some of their singles from *The Heist* on YouTube for free viewing. And Haggerty and Lewis created lots of hype about their music on social media sites including Instagram, Twitter, and Tumblr. Quillen's strategy worked. By April 2012 the single "Wing$" had 3 million views on YouTube.[2] It was time for the duo to step up to the next level.

|||||||||||||||||||||||||||||||||||||||||||||||||||||||

MARRIAGE EQUALITY

In the summer of 2012, officials in Washington State announced Referendum 74 would be on the fall ballot. The citizens would vote whether to legalize gay marriage in the state. On July 18, in the middle of the political debate about this referendum, Macklemore & Ryan Lewis released their single "Same Love." This song expresses the duo's belief gays and lesbians should have the same rights as everyone else.

Quillen insists they did not produce "Same Love" just because the country was in the right mood for a gay rights song. Both Lewis and Haggerty have relatives who are gay, and both men feel strongly about marriage equality. The song struck a popular chord, however, and the duo rode the wave. On October 11, 2012, talk show host Ellen DeGeneres tweeted a congratulatory message about how much she liked the song. On October 30, Haggerty and Lewis sang the song on her show, their first-ever television performance.

BEHIND "SAME LOVE"

Both Haggerty and Lewis have relatives who are gay. Lewis's uncle is gay and HIV-positive. Haggerty's uncle and godfather are both gay, as are many people in the liberal neighborhood where he grew up. As a third grader Haggerty remembered telling his mom he was worried he might be gay. His mom assured him it was okay and encouraged him to take ballet lessons with a peer who was being bullied for doing so. These influences went into the lyrics of "Same Love."

An August 2013 performance of "Same Love" on *Good Morning America* featured a same-sex couple's marriage proposal.

"THRIFT SHOP"

Next the team decided to promote "Thrift Shop," released on August 27. First they put the music video on YouTube, and then they hired Alternative Distribution Alliance (ADA) to persuade radio station executives the song was popular enough to play on the air. This was the first time the duo had hired an outside company to help them hype their music.

"Thrift Shop" is light and funny and easy to dance to. They wanted a song to counter the somber tone of "Same Love," but despite the fun lyrics, the message is honest. Haggerty has been a thrift shopper all his life. Lewis said when they go on tour, Haggerty usually visits at least 20 secondhand stores. He likes designer clothes too, but unusual used apparel is central to his style. By the fall of 2012, "Thrift Shop" had reached Number 15 on the *Billboard* rap singles chart, and the duo was playing sold-out shows across the country.

Then, amid all this hype, *The Heist* was released on October 9. Haggerty and Lewis guessed they might sell 20,000 copies. Instead, they sold a whopping 78,000, and the record reached Number 1 on iTunes charts and Number 2 on *Billboard* charts.[3] Because fans demanded it, independent radio stations began playing "Thrift Shop."

THANKS, BUT NO THANKS

On October 17, 2012, Macklemore & Ryan Lewis performed in Missoula, Montana, and music legend L. A. Reid showed up at the concert. Reid is the CEO of Epic Records, which is a division of Sony Music, one of the largest record labels. He offered

HIP-HOP IN THE 2000s

Several important changes occurred in hip-hop at the beginning of the 2000s. It was in the midst of these changes in the genre that Macklemore & Ryan Lewis released their debut album. Sales in the United States tumbled due to digital downloading; however, the growth of social media made it easy for anyone to post a song on video-sharing website YouTube and get noticed. The creative center of the genre moved to the southern United States. Groups such as Three 6 Mafia and Juvenile brought in the sounds of what is called the Dirty South. This new sound included regional styles. Rapper and producer Lil Jon developed crunk music, which includes lots of keyboard music and shouting. Bounce music came out of Louisiana and is known for its beat. Producers such as Dr. Dre and Timbaland became an important creative and commercial force. Their beats helped push hip-hop more into the mainstream.

to put all the resources of Epic and Sony behind promoting *The Heist* if Macklemore & Ryan Lewis signed a contract with Epic for their second album.

This was the moment most artists dream about. Someone inside the industry wanted to back them. Haggerty and Lewis turned down Reid. Haggerty explained why:

"Thrift Shop" became hugely popular in 2013 and got lots of radio airplay.

There's nothing a major [record label] could offer us that we can't do ourselves. . . . We're more fulfilled creatively. I'd much rather be 80 years old and say, "I've put out five albums that really meant something to me," than put out 50 that made a . . . load of money and didn't mean anything to me.[4]

Lewis's reasoning was similar:

Both of us get so much joy from the widespread creativity, not just the music, but the design that goes into your album art and tour merchandise. And, also not just from making music videos, but videos that promote different things and the way you want to make things feel. Those are all things we value.[5]

From Quillen's perspective, however, the problem with rejecting this deal was that the record labels control what music gets played on the radio. It is almost impossible to get a single played on mainstream radio without the backing of a major label's promotional team. Earlier in 2012, Quillen had cut a deal with ADA to distribute *The Heist*. ADA is an arm of Warner Brothers, another big record label. So Quillen returned to Warner Brothers and asked if he could hire the label's radio promoters directly without Macklemore & Ryan Lewis having to sign a contract with Warner Brothers. At first the company said no. It wanted to control the duo and profit from the group's success.

MAKING MUSIC HISTORY

Only twice in history has a song by an independent artist hit the Number 1 spot on *Billboard*'s Hot 100 hits. The first time was "Stay" by Lisa Loeb in 1994. The second time was "Thrift Shop" by Macklemore & Ryan Lewis in 2013. When "Can't Hold Us" (released in 2011) hit Number 1 on May 17, 2013, Macklemore & Ryan Lewis made *Billboard* history as the first duo to reach the top spot with their first two single releases. ("Same Love" is not included in this statistic because it was promoted only on alternative radio stations.)

Neither man is bound to one style of song. Macklemore & Ryan Lewis's music can be madcap one minute—think "Thrift Shop"—and serious the next, like "Same Love." They are open to pursuing whatever song or style feels genuine to them at a particular moment. Sometimes Haggerty will give Lewis lyrics and he'll build the music around the words, and other times it's the reverse process. The way the duo creates is constantly changing and evolving. Lewis believes this flexibility is unique in pop music, and it helps create great music that resonates with their fans.

However, Warner Brothers quickly reconsidered when it realized how popular the duo was becoming. Haggerty and Lewis signed with Warner Brothers to promote "Thrift Shop" on the radio. The song hit Number 1 on February 2, 2013.

A MUSIC INDUSTRY FIRST

Usually when a musician signs a contract with a major record label, the company puts out money up front for costs such as recording fees, video production, tour support, and radio and television promotion. However, in return they get a huge percentage of the profits from record sales and the right to future albums, as well as a share of merchandise sales, endorsements, and publishing contracts. The record labels get much richer than the musicians.

By contracting with Warner Brothers for just one service—radio promotion—Haggerty and Lewis charted new ground. It was the first time a major label agreed to promote a record without having signed a contract to represent the musicians in everything. This could be the beginning of a revolutionary shift in the way albums are marketed. Haggerty and Lewis were able to negotiate this kind of a deal because they already had tens of thousands of fans due to the quality of their music and their clever promotional strategy. And as 2012 gave way to 2013, the duo would be catapulted to a level of fame that seemed impossible just a few months earlier.

Macklemore & Ryan Lewis performed "Can't Hold Us" at the MTV Movie Awards on April 14, 2013. It was only the beginning of an epic year for the duo.

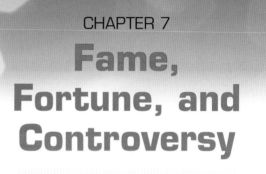

CHAPTER 7

Fame,
Fortune, and
Controversy

I n 2013, people took note of
Macklemore & Ryan Lewis. Their
music was hot. The industry
honored them, and the duo took their
songs to a world stage. In the spring
of 2013, the single "Can't Hold Us"
reached Number 1 on the *Billboard* Top
100 chart. Following the zany antics of
"Thrift Shop" and the serious tone of

Some commentators have objected to the message of "Same Love." One critic said the song implies black people, particularly hip-hop artists, are homophobic. He said it was wrong to assume gay people do not feel comfortable in the rap community. Other critics argued that instead of a straight rapper like Macklemore getting so much attention, the media should pay more attention to gay musicians.

"Same Love," this song was designed to appeal to a broader audience. The song tells the story of determination. Haggerty raps about how after chasing his dream since he was a teenager, he and Lewis have reached success by making music their way. Ray Dalton sings the song's hook: "Tonight is the night / we'll fight 'til it's over / So we put our hands up like the ceiling can't hold us."[1] Indeed, it seemed nothing could hold back the growing fame of Macklemore & Ryan Lewis.

||||||||||||||||||||||||||||||||||||||||||||||||||||

SELLING OUT

However, not all the attention the duo received was positive. In 2011, Macklemore & Ryan Lewis had released the single "Wing$." The song is about consumerism. Haggerty raps about how as a kid he wanted to be a great basketball player and dreamed the right shoes, specifically $200 Nikes, would help him soar. The song is a critique of a culture that pushes kids to feel less worthy, even worthless, if they do not look or dress a certain way. When "Wing$" was first released, the song did not receive much attention.

Then, in the winter of 2013, Macklemore & Ryan Lewis signed with the National Basketball Association (NBA) to perform an edited version of "Wing$" as part of a promotional video for the All-Star Game. A key line in the original song includes these lyrics: "Consumption is in the veins / And now I see it's just another pair of shoes."[2] The NBA makes a lot of money from athletic shoe sponsors. The line equating shoes with the evils of consumerism was cut. In the NBA's version of "Wings$," Haggerty sits on a basketball hoop and raps about how a pair of shoes would make him fly. The sanitized form of "Wing$" was about the love of basketball, not the dangers of consumerism.

There was backlash to this video. Commentators and some fans accused Macklemore & Ryan Lewis of selling out. Because the pair

Haggerty's home NBA team when he was growing up was the Seattle SuperSonics.

frequently state how proud they are to be independent from big corporations, it was jarring for some people to see "Wing$" being used by an institution such as the NBA.

Haggerty responded to this criticism. He said he has loved the NBA since he was a kid, and when he and Lewis were offered the chance to do the video, it was a "no-brainer." He knew the four-minute song would be edited down to 30 seconds but figured this editing was worth having the video be seen by millions of people. If they liked the song enough, Haggerty hoped they would listen to the entire version of "Wing$" and maybe other songs as well. He explained further:

In my stripped down definition, selling out is compromising your artistic integrity for money/fame. In my heart I can tell you that my personal artistic integrity remained completely intact. . . . They picked the parts that fit their ad campaign, and visually matched it to us performing, threw in a highlight reel of crazy dunks and had a bunch of kids singing the hook in a gym. Word. I'm all for that. If you take away the consumerism cautionary core of Wings, a story still remains. And that story is one that I'm still proud of.[3]

FROM PIRATE SHIPS TO
SOCIAL MESSAGES

Throughout the summer of 2013, Macklemore & Ryan Lewis drew national attention. They garnered a slew of nominations for the MTV Video Music Awards. When the awards night arrived in August, they walked away with two prestigious honors: Best Hip-Hop Video for "Can't Hold Us" and Best Video with a Social Message for "Same Love."

The music video for "Can't Hold Us" was shot on two continents. It features a pack of huskies, a camel, a pirate ship, and the cherub-cheeked Ray Dalton belting out his baritone. It ends with a flag labeled *The Heist* flying from the Space Needle in Seattle. This video showcases the group's over-the-top, flamboyant side.

Haggerty, Lewis, Mary Lambert, and guest singer Jennifer Hudson performed "Same Love" at the MTV Video Music Awards. Lambert, who is a lesbian, said, "It's really incredible to be a part of such an incredible social movement and to have the support and to go around the world and say, 'What's up? I'm gay,' and have everyone's support."[4]

|||||||||||||||||||||||||||||||||||||||||||||||||||||||||||

Lambert, Haggerty, and Lewis accepted the MTV Video Music Award for Best Video with a Social Message.

ON THE ROAD

To cap off their year, Haggerty and Lewis took their show on the road. On September 9, they started their Fall World Tour in London, England. Fans who wanted to see the behind-the-scenes action of this 90-date tour could watch a five-part documentary on YouTube. Filmmaker Buffalo David Bitton tagged along with the duo all over Europe and back to the United States. The documentary begins with a close-up on Wanz's face. He says, "Something interesting is about to happen here. I bet you can't wait to see what it is."[5] The fans are drawn in.

From London to Zurich to Paris, the camera shows adoring crowds screaming at concerts, Lewis

IN TRAINING

Touring is exhausting. All members of the crew work hard over long hours. For Haggerty, the physical demands are especially intense because he must rap and dance on stage for hours each night. In preparation for a tour, Haggerty runs, does breathing exercises, and lifts weights. He says, "If my voice goes, then the tour goes. So as always, I need to make sure my voice is right, I'm physically fit, and I'm mentally in a place where I'm going to be giving everything I have for 60+ days in a row."[6]

Haggerty crowd dives during many of his live performances.

wringing the sweat from his T-shirt after a show, and Haggerty giving a pep talk to stagehands. The viewer feels like a member of the crew when Lewis leans into the camera and whispers some fact about where they are at a particular moment. The documentary is an intimate way to connect with fans. On this tour Europe fell in love with the

In an interview, Haggerty described what goes on in his head during a concert. He said that at worst, he feels mad—maybe at the crowd, maybe at Lewis, maybe because he knows he should not have eaten a cheeseburger earlier. At best, he feels present and glad to be with his fans. Sometimes Haggerty crowd surfs because he is frustrated with his audience and decides to jump into them and "flail around and take out my aggression and try to hype them up." Other times he dives into a crowd because he is so happy he just wants to get a big crowd hug. Once in Beirut, Lebanon, Haggerty jumped into a crowd and they dropped him. "It can get a little bit scary out there sometimes," he said.[7]

duo. Rebecca Chung Filice plays cello in the band. She said fans lined up for 24 hours to try to get seats closest to the stage.

RAP AND RACE

In November 2013, Macklemore & Ryan Lewis were honored with more accolades. This time it was the American Music Award for Favorite Rap/Hip-Hop Album. Haggerty and Lewis appeared via live feed from Florida. True to form, Haggerty used the spotlight to address an important issue—race.

In Florida in 2012, 17-year-old Trayvon Martin was shot and killed by George Zimmerman while Martin was walking home from a convenience store. The trial was racially charged because Martin was an unarmed African-American teenager and Zimmerman was white and had a gun. The jury found Zimmerman not guilty for Martin's death because they were convinced Zimmerman believed his own life was in danger.

With Lewis by his side, Haggerty chose to address this emotionally charged issue when he accepted the American Music Award:

> Due to the fact that we are in Florida tonight accepting this award, I want to acknowledge Trayvon Martin and the hundreds and hundreds of kids each year that are dying due to racial profiling and the violence that follows it. . . . These are our friends, our neighbors, our peers and our fans, and it's time that we look out for

AWARDS APLENTY |||||||||||||||||||||||||||||||||||||||||||||||||||||||||||||||||||||||||

The honors that piled on Macklemore & Ryan Lewis in 2013 make a long list. The hip-hop duo was nominated for 58 awards in both the United States and Europe, and they won 14.[8]

There are people who object to both the song "Same Love" and the issue of gay marriage. In 2012, a middle school teacher in Detroit, Michigan, was suspended for playing the song for her eighth-grade performing arts class. In 2013, a North Carolina teacher was suspended after she showed the "Same Love" music video to her students. Administrators questioned whether the song and video were age appropriate and relevant to the curriculum. Following the first incident, Haggerty wrote on his blog that "Same Love" was written "with the hope that it would facilitate dialogue and through those conversations understanding and empathy would emerge."[10] Both teachers were back to work within a couple of days.

the youth and fight against racism and the laws that protect it.[9]

The duo once again proved they were not afraid to take a political stance on controversial issues, unconcerned about how it might affect their music sales.

A few weeks later it was December 6, 2013, the night of the Grammy Nominations Concert. Macklemore & Ryan Lewis performed "Thrift Shop," and they were nominated for seven Grammys. As 2013 drew to a close, they waited for

Haggerty and Wanz strutted down the aisle to the stage at the Grammy Nominations Concert.

the Grammy Awards ceremony, where they would discover whether they would be honored with the most prestigious award a musician can earn.

Haggerty and Lewis arrive at the
Grammy Awards with their dates.

CHAPTER 8

Grammy Night

O n the evening of January 26, 2014, two couples posed on the red carpet that leads into the Staples Center in Los Angeles. Haggerty wore a dark teal suit with a black bowtie. His fiancée, Tricia Davis, struck a pose in a floor-length white gown. Lewis, normally a conservative dresser, sported a gray-and-black houndstooth check suit. His date, Jackie Granger, was also bold, dressed in a canary yellow, backless gown. Despite their finery, as the photographers clicked away, the hip-hop duo looked nervous. The men's smiles were tight, as though they wanted to get out of the spotlight. However, they would have to wait. On this night, the spotlight would shine directly on them.

||||||||||||||||||||||||||||||||||||||||||||||||||||||

HONORS

The Recording Academy gives out dozens of Grammy Awards that are not telecast on national television because the ceremony would simply take too long. So starting at 1:00 p.m. on January 26, the less well-known awards were given. These included honors such as Best Surround Sound Album and Best Tropical Latin Album. Many artists, particularly the big names and those performing in the evening ceremony, did not show up to receive their awards in person. Haggerty and Lewis garnered three Grammys in the early ceremony: Best Rap Performance, Best Rap Song, and Best Rap Album. Anyone would call that a success, but the evening was not yet over.

||||||||||||||||||||||||||||||||||||||||||||||||||||||

> "First and foremost being true to who you are. Finding your own voice. Being authentic. . . . We are all individuals. We are all people who have our own unique story. . . . It's a disservice to try to copy others."[1]
>
> —HAGGERTY'S ADVICE FOR YOUNG HIP-HOPPERS

NEW KIDS ON THE BLOCK

One of the most anticipated moments of the Grammy Awards ceremony is the announcement of Best New Artist. This musician, or musicians, must have released a recording the previous year that established a public identity. Although Haggerty had been making music for years, he was not well known until *The Heist* was released at the end of 2012, and Lewis was a virtual unknown before the album came out.

Early in the televised ceremony, a presenter read the names of the artists contending for Best New Artist of 2013: James Blake, Kendrick Lamar, Macklemore & Ryan Lewis, Kacey Musgraves, and Ed Sheeran. There was a pause.

Lewis and Haggerty accept their award for Best New Artist.

Then the presenter said, "And the Grammy goes to . . ."[2] There was another long pause.

The television camera panned over each competitor's face. Haggerty and Lewis sat side by side. Haggerty blinked rapidly, his eyes fixed on the stage. Lewis leaned forward slightly, his head turned to one side as though uninterested.

Then the winner was announced: Macklemore & Ryan Lewis.

As the two men kissed their dates and walked toward the stage, the chorus of "Can't Hold Us" boomed throughout the auditorium. Haggerty held the trophy while Lewis stood beside him. "Whooo!" Haggerty said, releasing a loud sigh. "First and foremost, I want to thank our fans."[3] Then he repeated the fact that has been widely reported and admired about Macklemore & Ryan Lewis. They made *The Heist* without a record label. They made it independently. Lewis raised his hand in the air, and the two men left the stage to cheers and applause.

WEDDED BLISS

Macklemore & Ryan Lewis did not get any more Grammys that evening, but their time on stage was not over. A little later, rapper and actress Queen Latifah introduced them and said they would be performing a love song, not "for some of us, but for all of us."[4] The song, of course, was "Same Love." Haggerty and Lewis had performed this ballad countless times in the last year, before audiences around the world. But this time it would be different.

Haggerty rapped the story of how in third grade he thought he might be gay because his uncle was.

Then Mary Lambert's soaring soprano came in with the hook, "I can't change, even if I tried. Even if I wanted to," accompanied by Trombone Shorty's peals on the horn.[5] Halfway through the song, mock cathedral doors behind Haggerty opened up and Queen Latifah reentered the stage and said, "We are gathered here to celebrate love and harmony."[6]

In two lines along the front of the auditorium, 33 couples, some same-sex and some of opposite genders, faced each other. Queen Latifah told the couples to exchange rings, and then she pronounced them "a married couple."[7] The crowd roared.

While "Same Love" was still playing, pop star Madonna entered through the cathedral doors, dressed in a white suit and white cowboy hat.

YOU CAN PLAY

In 2014, Macklemore & Ryan Lewis released a video for a public service announcement for the You Can Play organization. This new group is dedicated to helping create an environment where kids can participate in sports safely and positively, regardless of their sexual orientation. In the video, Macklemore tells kids antigay language has no place in sports or music. "If you can play, you can play."[8]

Haggerty and Lewis took the Grammy stage with Lambert, Madonna, and Queen Latifah.

She joined the conclusion of the song, singing her 1986 hit "Open Your Heart." The now married couples wept and embraced. A choir harmonized with Madonna as Lewis worked the sound machines and sang along from the back of the stage. The newly married couples included his sister and her new husband.

As the couples exited the auditorium, the voices of Madonna and Lambert blended into an emotional crescendo. As the final notes fell, Haggerty, Lambert, Madonna, Lewis, and Queen Latifah stood arm in arm on center stage. A teary audience gave them a standing ovation.

REACTION TO THEIR WIN

When interviewed following the ceremony, Lewis described winning a Grammy as "crazy." He said no musician thinks he'll ever win a Grammy. Lewis waved his hand in the air like he was indicating an impossible dream. Then he said achieving this honor was the "apex" and the "pinnacle."[9]

While Haggerty was excited too, he also experienced a different reaction—guilt. Weeks before the awards ceremony, Haggerty had said in an interview that the hip-hop community would be angry if *The Heist* took home the award for Best Rap Album. He said, "We're up against Kendrick [Lamar], who made a phenomenal album. If we win a Grammy for Best Rap Album, hip-hop is going to be heated."[10] He was proud of *The Heist* but felt rapper Kendrick Lamar's album was a better *rap* album.

Haggerty's prediction came true. Macklemore & Ryan Lewis beat out Lamar for Best Rap Album. Following the ceremony, Haggerty sent a text message to Lamar. "You got robbed. I wanted you to win."[11] Then Haggerty posted the text on Instagram. Some people criticized this as a publicity stunt, but Lamar accepted the gesture as genuine.

Haggerty suffered winner's guilt. In an interview the day after the Grammys, he called the awards a blessing and a curse. The curse was that he and Lewis had beaten out Lamar, a musician Haggerty admires. Haggerty believed he and Lewis had an unfair advantage because they are white and Lamar is African American. He seemed to imply their win for Best Rap Album was an act of unconscious racism on the part of the people who voted for them. These members of the Academy who select the Grammy winners come from all musical

HIP-HOP ENOUGH

Macklemore & Ryan Lewis have taken some heat for not being hip-hop enough. Haggerty acknowledged this in an interview shortly before the 2014 Grammy Awards. He said, "People are going to be skeptical. I'm a white dude from Seattle. People are rightfully skeptical of white people making hip-hop."[12]

But he believes the skepticism is because of the popularity of "Thrift Shop." Haggerty maintains that people listened to that one song and pegged him and Lewis as pop artists. They did not listen to the rest of the songs on the album. He said, "You take the race thing out . . . you cannot deny the quality of the music."[13]

backgrounds. Haggerty believed those voters who were not rap fans cast their ballot for the white guys whose song they heard so much on the radio—"Thrift Shop."

The media gave a lot of attention to Haggerty's text message. Lewis eventually entered the conversation and said, "I think, very plain and simple, we made an album we're super proud of and which resonated with [hundreds and thousands] of people. But we're also a huge fan of Kendrick Lamar. We just acknowledged that we love (Kendrick's) album."[14]

||||||||||||||||||||||||||||||||||||||||||||||||||||||||||

SPEAKING UP FOR NATURE ||||||||||||||||||||||||||||||||||||||||||||||||||||||

The Nature Conservancy is an organization that works to preserve nature. Haggerty and Lewis appeared on a video spot for the organization in which they spoke about the beauty of the state of Washington. Lewis described the scenic Cascade Mountains and other "epic surroundings" that fueled their musical creativity. Haggerty talked about growing up in the 1980s when technology was limited and the kids in his neighborhood "kicked it" outside, something he thinks kids today should get back to.[15] The use of celebrities is one way to attract more youths to the work the Nature Conservancy does to protect the environment.

WHAT'S NEXT?

Shortly after the Grammy Awards, Macklemore & Ryan Lewis hit the road again. They finished a tour of Australia and Asia, had a brief break at home, and then headed to Dubai in the United Arab Emirates in the spring of 2014.

Plans for recording another album are definitely on the horizon, but both Lewis and Haggerty insist they will take their time. *The Heist* took three years to produce. Lewis said with the next record, "We'll take as long as we need to, and work really hard to get it right."[16]

Although he loves making music, Lewis has other dreams as well. He would like to eventually direct movies, perhaps even do some acting. Another one of his passions is film scoring. He is young, talented, and motivated, and the future is wide open.

Haggerty's plans seem closer to home. Knowing he is financially set for life gives him a sense of relief. He also finally feels accepted by the hip-hop community. One concern that hangs over Haggerty's future is the danger of a relapse. In early January 2014, he admitted that when he comes off

The future looks bright for the Grammy-winning duo.

the road from a tour, the temptation to use drugs and alcohol is very strong. In a 2013 interview, Haggerty explained one strategy for staying sober. "I can say that right now, I'm sober. I plan on remaining sober for the rest of the day. And starting over again tomorrow."[17]

Both men seem relatively settled. Haggerty is engaged to longtime girlfriend Tricia Davis and in 2014 they were considering starting a family soon.

Lewis too seemed to be putting down roots, buying a multimillion-dollar home in Seattle.

No matter what the future holds, Haggerty and Lewis want to continue making good music. Haggerty has said music is the foundation for everything: "It comes down to making records, making music for the right reasons, remembering why we love to make art and just doing it. Everything else will fall into place."[18]

THE HALF OF US

The Jed Foundation and MTV combined forces to produce a 12-part video campaign designed to help college students understand and cope with the problem of prescription drug abuse. Haggerty kicked off the campaign on January 30, 2014, with an intimate interview in which he speaks bluntly about the dangers of OxyContin. "Oxy is the most intense drug. . . . I mean it's synthetic heroin . . . that's the definition of it."[19] Haggerty chokes up when he tells the story of a rapper friend who died from an overdose of OxyContin. The Half of Us website offers resources for college students struggling with drug abuse and alcohol addiction. Bulleted checklists of symptoms let readers know what addiction looks like. There are tips for preventing addiction, as well as suggestions for helping struggling friends. In addition to Haggerty, several celebrities and college students are interviewed on the Half of Us website.

TIMELINE

1983
1988
2000

Ben Haggerty is born on June 19 in Seattle, Washington.

Ryan Lewis is born on March 25 in Spokane, Washington.

Haggerty spends the summer in New York City and creates the character Professor Macklemore.

2008
2009
2009

Haggerty goes to rehab for alcohol and drug addiction.

Haggerty releases *The Unplanned Mixtape* EP.

Lewis graduates from the University of Washington.

2004

Haggerty records his first single, "Welcome to Myspace."

2005

Haggerty and Josh Karp release the album *The Language of My World*.

2006

Haggerty and Lewis first meet on Myspace.

2009

Haggerty and Lewis collaborate to produce the EP titled *VS*, and Macklemore officially becomes Macklemore & Ryan Lewis.

2011

Zach Quillen becomes the manager of Macklemore & Ryan Lewis.

2012

On July 18, the single "Same Love" is released.

TIMELINE

2012

On August 27, the single "Thrift Shop" is released.

2012

On October 9, Macklemore & Ryan Lewis release their first full-length album, *The Heist*.

2012

On October 17, the CEO of Epic Records offers to represent Macklemore & Ryan Lewis, but they turn him down.

2013

On May 17, "Can't Hold Us" reaches Number 1 on the *Billboard* Hot 100; Macklemore & Ryan Lewis become the first duo to have their first two singles reach Number 1 status.

2013

On September 9, Macklemore & Ryan Lewis kick off *The Heist* world tour with a concert in London.

2013

On December 6, Macklemore & Ryan Lewis are nominated for seven Grammy Awards.

2012	2013	2013

On October 30, Macklemore & Ryan Lewis perform for the first time on television on *The Ellen DeGeneres Show*.

Haggerty and girlfriend Tricia Davis get engaged in January.

On February 2, "Thrift Shop" reaches Number 1 on the *Billboard* Hot 100.

2014	2014	2014

On January 26, Macklemore & Ryan Lewis win four Grammy Awards.

On January 30, Haggerty premiers a 12-spot public service video to combat prescription drug abuse.

On April 22, Ryan Lewis announces his mother is HIV-positive and launches the 30/30 Project.

GET THE SCOOP

FULL NAME

Ben Haggerty

DATE OF BIRTH

June 19, 1983

PLACE OF BIRTH

Seattle, Washington

FULL NAME

Ryan Lewis

DATE OF BIRTH

March 25, 1988

PLACE OF BIRTH

Spokane, Washington

EPS AND ALBUMS

VS (2009), *VS. Redux* (2010), *The Heist* (2012)

SELECTED TOURS

Fall World Tour (2013)

SELECTED AWARDS

- Won the *Billboard* Music Award Rap Song of the Year for "Thrift Shop" in 2013
- Won the *Billboard* Music Award Top Rap Song for "Can't Hold Us" in 2014
- Won Best New Artist at the Grammy Awards in 2014
- Won Best Rap Album for *The Heist* at the Grammy Awards in 2014
- Won Best Rap Performance and Best Rap Song for "Thrift Shop" at the Grammy Awards in 2014
- First duo to reach the Number 1 spot on the *Billboard* Hot 100 chart with their first two singles

PHILANTHROPY

Ryan Lewis began the 30/30 Project with his family in 2014, and Ben Haggerty has lent his support. The foundation builds medical centers in poor countries. Haggerty is involved in antidrug and proequality organizations.

"It comes down to making records, making music for the right reasons, remembering why we love to make art and just doing it. Everything else will fall into place."

—BEN HAGGERTY (MACKLEMORE)

GLOSSARY

beat—An instrumental track created by using a sample from an already recorded song.

Billboard—A music chart system used by the music recording industry to measure record popularity and sales.

break—A short musical passage in which all musicians except one fall silent.

break dance—A form of dance that started in the 1970s, is performed to rap music, and is characterized by fancy footwork, tumbling, and spinning on the head and back.

chart—A weekly listing of songs or albums in order of popularity or record sales.

consumerism—The belief that it is a good thing when people spend a lot of money on products and services.

DJ—A person who announces or plays popular recorded music.

extended play (EP)—A musical release with more than one song or track, but not enough for an album.

Grammy Award—One of several awards the National Academy of Recording Arts and Sciences presents each year to honor musical achievement.

hip-hop—A style of popular music associated with American urban culture that features rap spoken against a background of electronic music or beats.

indie rap—Experimental hip-hop music.

mantra—A word or sound that is repeated in order to enhance meditation.

MC—Standing for master of ceremonies in the world of hip-hop; a rapper or one who controls the stage.

meditation—The act of focusing one's mind for a period of time either for relaxation or spiritual purposes.

producer—Someone who oversees or provides money for a play, television show, movie, or album.

rap—A style of popular music noted for rhythmic speaking of rhymed couplets set to a strong beat.

record label—A brand or trademark related to the marketing of music videos and recordings.

sampling—The process of using prerecorded sounds to create a new piece of music.

single—An individual song that is distributed on its own over the radio and other mediums.

synthesizer—A machine that uses amplifiers and filters to create sound electronically.

turntable—A device that plays a vinyl record. DJs often move a record back and forth to create a popular "scratching" sound.

ADDITIONAL RESOURCES

SELECTED BIBLIOGRAPHY

Hiatt, Brian. "393 Million Macklemore (And Ryan Lewis!) Fans Can't Be Wrong." *Rolling Stone* 1190 (2013): 40–70. *Academic Search Premier*. Web. 24 Apr. 2014.

"Ryan Lewis: 'I've Never Looked at Myself as a Beat Maker.'" *XXL Magazine*. Harris Publications, 22 Mar. 2013. Web. 24 Apr. 2014.

Varga, George. "Macklemore & Ryan Lewis: The Stars Align." U-T San Diego. San Diego Union Tribune, 29 Nov. 2013. Web. 1 May 2014.

Vozick-Levinson, Simon. "Thrift Shop Hero." *Rolling Stone* 1180 (2013): 48–51. *Academic Search Premier*. Web. 24 Apr. 2014.

FURTHER READINGS

Giovanni, Nikki. *Hip Hop Speaks to Children: A Celebration of Poetry with a Beat*. Naperville, IL: Sourcebooks, Jabberwocky, 2008. Print.

Merino, Noel. *Rap Music: Introducing Issues with Opposing Viewpoints*. Farmington Hills, MI: Greenhaven, 2008. Print.

WEBSITES

To learn more about Contemporary Lives, visit **booklinks.abdopublishing.com**. These links are routinely monitored and updated to provide the most current information available.

PLACES TO VISIT

Grammy Museum
800 W. Olympic Boulevard
Los Angeles, CA 90015
http://www.grammymuseum.org
213-765-6800
This museum in downtown Los Angeles has exhibits on
four floors that cover many aspects of musical history,
including technology, the creative process, and the history
of the Grammy Awards.

Hip-Hop Hall of Fame Museum and Entertainment Complex
http://hiphophof.tv
This museum is under development and is scheduled
to open in late 2015. It will be located in Midtown
Manhattan. The complex will include the Hip-Hop Hall of
Fame Museum, stores, restaurants, a concert lounge, and
television studios.

Space Needle
400 Broad Street
Seattle, WA 98109
http://www.spaceneedle.com/home
206-905-2100
View the city where Macklemore & Ryan Lewis first got
their start from 520 feet off the ground on the observation
deck of the Seattle Space Needle.

SOURCE NOTES

CHAPTER 1. NOMINATED

1. "Song Of The Year Nominees." *Grammy.com*. The Recording Academy, 6 Dec. 2013. Web. 21 Apr. 2014.

2. Ibid.

3. "Macklemore & Ryan Lewis—Thrift Shop (Grammy Nominations Concert)." *The Hollywood Gossip*. Celebrity Gossip and Entertainment News, 7 Dec. 2013. Web. 24 Apr. 2014.

4. "Macklemore & Ryan Lewis: Grammy Noms Concert Backstage." *Grammy.com*. The Recording Academy, 6 Dec. 2013. Web. 24 Apr. 2014.

5. Ibid.

6. "Macklemore & Ryan Lewis on Grammy Nomination Concert." *CBS News*. CBS News, 7 Dec. 2014. Web. 24 Apr. 2014.

CHAPTER 2. RAISED ON RAP

1. Marisa Fox. "The Heist Crew." *Billboard* 125.49 (2013): 17. *Academic Search Premier*. Web. 24 Apr. 2014.

2. Casey Jarman. "Mack to the Future." *Willamette Week*. Willamette Week Newspaper, 7 Sept. 2011. Web. 28 Apr. 2014.

3. Ibid.

4. Ibid.

5. "Macklemore and Ryan Lewis—Vipassana Lyrics." *Rap Genius*. Genius Media Group, n.d. Web. 29 Apr. 2014.

6. Professor Macklemore. "Welcome to the Culture." *Rap Genius*. Genius Media Group, n.d. Web. 23 May 2014.

CHAPTER 3. A BOY FROM MIDDLE AMERICA

1. "'You're Just Fearful!' Ryan Lewis Reveals How He Grew Up Worrying His HIV Positive Mother Julie Would Die." *Mail Online*. Daily Mail, 1 May 2014. Web. 23 May 2014.

2. "Macklemore & Ryan Lewis Star Opens Up about His Mom's HIV Survival." *CBS This Morning*. CBS News, 23 Apr. 2014. Web. 30 Apr. 2014.

3. Seth Sommerfield. "A Different Beat." *Inlander*. Inlander, 26 Feb. 2013. Web. 24 Apr. 2014.

4. Ibid.

5. "Ryan Lewis: 'I've Never Looked at Myself as a Beat Maker.'" *XXL Magazine*. Harris Publications. 22 Mar. 2013. Web. 24 Apr. 2014.

CHAPTER 4. COLLEGE YEARS

1. Brad Nehring. "Seattleite Spotlight: Hip-Hop Icon Macklemore." *Seattleite*. Seattleite, 4 Oct. 2012. Web. 24 Apr. 2014.

2. Gregory Lobo-Jost. "Music Programs in Prisons." *Encyclopedia of Prisons & Correctional Facilities*. SAGE Reference Online, 1 Aug. 2012. Web. 1 May 2014.

3. Todd Hamm. "Music. Drugs. God. Music." *City Arts*. Encore Media Group, 1 Dec. 2009. Web. 29 Apr. 2014.

4. Ibid.

5. Ibid.

6. Ibid.

7. Ibid.

8. George Varga. "Macklemore & Ryan Lewis: The Stars Align." *U-T San Diego*. San Diego Union Tribune, 29 Nov. 2013. Web. 1 May 2014.

CHAPTER 5. MAKING *THE HEIST*

1. Brian Hiatt. "393 Million Macklemore (And Ryan Lewis!) Fans Can't Be Wrong." *Rolling Stone* 1190 (2013): 40–70. *Academic Search Premier*. Web. 24 Apr. 2014.

2. Carolyn Lamberson. "Macklemore & Ryan Lewis Found History-Making Global Success." *The Spokesman-Review*. Spokesman-Review, 31 May 2013. Web. 3 May 2014.

3. "Macklemore—Otherside Lyrics." *RapGenius*. Genius Media Group, n.d. Web. 3 May 2014.

4. George Varga. "Macklemore & Ryan Lewis: The Stars Align." *U-T San Diego*. San Diego Union Tribune, 29 Nov. 2013. Web. 1 May 2014.

5. "Exclusive Interview: Macklemore and Ryan Lewis at the Bowery." *Respect Magazine*. Respect, 9 Dec. 2011. Web. 1 May 2014.

6. George Varga. "Macklemore & Ryan Lewis: The Stars Align." *U-T San Diego*. San Diego Union Tribune, 29 Nov. 2013. Web. 1 May 2014.

7. Brian Hiatt. "393 Million Macklemore (And Ryan Lewis!) Fans Can't Be Wrong." *Rolling Stone* 1190 (2013): 40–70. *Academic Search Premier*. Web. 24 Apr. 2014.

8. Dan Buyanovsky. "Macklemore and Ryan Lewis Find Clarity." *Interview Magazine*. Interview Magazine, n.d. Web. 24 Apr. 2014.

CHAPTER 6. GOING IT ALONE

1. "How Was the Name Sharkface Gang Created?" *NW Hip-Hop.* NW Hip-Hop, 9 Oct. 2012. Web. 4 May 2014.

2. Solveig Whittle. "The Secrets of Marketing Macklemore & Ryan Lewis' 'The Heist' from Manager Zach Quillen." *Hypebot.com.* Hypebot, 9 Apr. 2014. Web. 4 May 2014.

3. Seth Sommerfield. "A Different Beat." *Inlander.* Inlander, 26 Feb. 2013. Web. 24 Apr. 2014.

4. Marisa Fox. "M&RL: Doing It on Their Own." *Billboard* 125.20 (2013): 20–23. *Academic Search Premier.* Web. 24 Apr. 2014.

5. George Varga. "Macklemore & Ryan Lewis: The Stars Align." *U-T San Diego.* San Diego Union Tribune, 29 Nov. 2013. Web. 1 May 2014.

CHAPTER 7. FAME, FORTUNE, AND CONTROVERSY

1. "Macklemore & Ryan Lewis: Can't Hold Us." *YouTube.* YouTube, 17 Apr. 2013. Web. 4 May 2014.

2. Jordan Teicher. "Macklemore's Strangely Self-Censored NBA Promo." *Slate.com.* Slate Group, 15 Feb. 2013. Web. 4 May 2014.

3. Macklemore. "WINGS, THE NBA ALL-STAR GAME, & SELLING OUT." *Macklemore.com.* Macklemore and Ryan Lewis, 21 Feb. 2013. Web. 4 May 2014.

4. Rob Markman. "'Same Love' Sparked 'Incredible Movement,' Mary Lambert Gushes." *MTV News.* Viacom, 27 Aug. 2013. Web. 4 May 2014.

5. "Macklemore & Ryan Lewis: Fall Tour Documentary Series." *YouTube.* YouTube, 3 Oct. 2013. Web. 5 May 2014.

6. Brad Nehring. "Seattleite Spotlight: Hip-Hop Icon Macklemore." *Seattleite.* Seattleite, 4 Oct. 2012. Web. 24 Apr. 2014.

7. "What I'm Thinking When I'm Onstage." *Rolling Stone* 1189 (2013): 50. *Academic Search Premier.* Web. 5 May 2014.

8. "Macklemore Awards." *AceShowBiz.* AceShowBiz.com, n.d. Web. 5 May 2014.

9. "American Music Awards 2013: Macklemore & Ryan Lewis an Early Winner, Offer Tribute to Trayvon Martin." *Syracuse.com.* Syracuse Media Group, 24 Nov. 2013. Web. 4 May 2014.

10. Alan Duke and Joe Sutton. "Teacher Suspended for Showing Class Macklemore's 'Same Love' Video." *CNN Entertainment.* CNN, 12 Sept. 2013. Web. 5 May 2014.

CHAPTER 8. GRAMMY NIGHT

1. Jack Rome. "Amazing Mentor: Spotlight Interview with Macklemore." *Amazing Mentor*. Amazing Kids, Feb. 2012. Web. 24 Apr. 2014.

2. "Macklemore & Ryan Lewis Win Best New Artist." *Grammy.com*. Recording Academy, 26 Jan. 2014. Web. 5 May 2014.

3. Ibid.

4. "Macklemore & Ryan Lewis—'Same Love' Grammy's 2014." *YouTube*. YouTube, 1 Feb. 2014. Web. 5 May 2014.

5. Ibid.

6. Ibid.

7. Ibid.

8. J. R. Tungol. "Macklemore And Ryan Lewis Release 'You Can Play' PSA To Combat Homophobia in Sports." *Huffington Post*. Huffington Post, 27 Feb. 2013. Web. 5 May 2014.

9. "Macklemore & Ryan Lewis: Winning Four GRAMMYs Is Crazy." *Grammy.com*. Recording Academy, 26 Jan. 2014. Web. 5 May 2014.

10. Nadeska Alexis. "Exclusive: Macklemore Is *The Source*'s Man Of The Year." *MTV News*. Viacom, 7 Jan. 2014. Web. 5 May 2014.

11. Jason Newman. "Kendrick Lamar Praises Macklemore's Apologetic Grammy Text." *Rolling Stone*. Rolling Stone, 28 Feb. 2014. Web. 5 May 2014.

12. Nadeska Alexis. "Exclusive: Macklemore Is *The Source*'s Man Of The Year." *MTV News*. Viacom, 7 Jan. 2014. Web. 5 May 2014.

13. Ibid.

14. Nathalie Tomada. "Fresh from Their Grammy Wins: Macklemore & Ryan Lewis Coming to Manila." *Philstar.com*. Philippine Star, 25 Feb. 2014. Web. 5 May 2014.

15. "Macklemore & Ryan Lewis Interviewed on Growing Up in Seattle's Outdoors." *Nature Conservancy*. Nature Conservancy, 2014. Web. 5 May 2014.

16. Caitlyn Davey. "Macklemore and Ryan Lewis Interview." *Time Out Abu Dhabi*. ITP Digital, 15 Apr. 2014. Web. 23 May 2014.

17. Simon Vozick-Levinso. "Thrift Shop Hero." *Rolling Stone* 1180 (2013): 48–51. *Academic Search Premier*. Web. 24 Apr. 2014.

18. Steven J. Horowitz. "Stick-Up Kids." *Billboard* 124.38 (2012): 30. *Academic Search Premier*. Web. 24 Apr. 2014.

19. Nadeska Alexis. "Macklemore Gets Candid about Drug Addiction That Almost Ruined Music Career." *MTV News*. Viacom, 30 Jan. 2014. Web. 28 Apr. 2014.

INDEX

American Music Awards, 79–80
"And We Danced," 44, 49
Arunga, Owuor, 10–11

Bitton, Buffalo David, 76–77
Budo, 37–39, 42

"Can't Hold Us," 13, 65, 69–70, 74, 86–87
city bus performance, 13
"Claiming the City," 18

Dalton, Ray, 53, 70, 74
Davis, Tricia, 40, 53, 83, 94
Digital Underground, 17, 18
Drake, 8

Elevated Elements, 21
Epic Records, 62–63

*F*ake Empire, 45

Gateways, 35, 36
Granger, Jackie, 83–84

Haggerty, Ben
addiction, 20, 21, 37, 39, 40, 41–42, 48, 49, 94, 95
childhood, 17–19
college, 35–39
engagement, 40, 94
meditation, 20, 43–44
musical influences, 17, 21
rehabilitation, 42–44
siblings, 18
style, 21–22, 61–62
teen years, 20–23
training, 76
See also Macklemore & Ryan Lewis
Haggerty, Bill (father of Ben Haggerty), 18, 42
Half of Us, 94
Heist, The, 9, 47–50, 52–54, 57, 59, 62, 63, 65, 74, 85, 87, 90, 93
hip-hop, 12, 22, 30, 31, 32, 63, 90, 91
HIV, 26–29, 60
"Humpty Dance, The," 17, 18

Jed Foundation, 95

Karp, Josh. *See* Budo

Lamar, Kendrick, 85, 90–92
Lambert, Mary, 53, 74, 88–89
Language of My World, The, 37

Lewis, Julie (mother of Ryan
    Lewis), 25, 26–29, 31
Lewis, Ryan
    childhood, 25–30
    college, 39–41, 44–45
    musical influences, 29–31
    One Example, 30
    other interests, 39, 44–45,
        52–54, 93
    Schema, 31
    siblings, 26, 29, 89
    teen years, 30–32
    See also Macklemore &
        Ryan Lewis
Lewis, Scott (father of Ryan
    Lewis), 25–26, 29, 31
LL Cool J, 8, 22
Lorde, 8, 12

Macklemore & Ryan Lewis
    awards, 74, 76, 78, 79, 84,
        85–87, 90–92
    controversy, 69–73, 74,
        78–81, 90–92
    creative process, 50,
        52–54, 66
    fan club (see Shark Face
        Gang)
    meeting, 39–41, 47–48
    nominations, 8, 9, 12–13,
        74, 79, 80

philanthropy, 28, 88, 92
promotional strategy,
    58–59, 61–62, 63–65,
    66–67
social media, 37, 59, 63
social messages, 59–60,
    74, 78–81
tour documentary, 76–78
touring, 58, 59, 76–78, 93
Madonna, 88–89
marriage equality, 59–60, 80
Mars, Bruno, 8
Martin, Trayvon, 79–80
Miguel, 12
MTV, 95
MTV Video Music Awards,
    74
"Music Unleashes Us," 13
music videos, 49, 53, 59,
    61, 64, 74, 80
Myspace, 37, 39, 40, 48

National Basketball
    Association, 71–73
Nature Conservancy, 92
New York City, 13, 21, 22

Open Your Eyes, 22–23
"Otherside," 48–49
OxyContin, 42, 95

Perry, Katy, 8
Pink, 8

Queen Latifah, 87–89
Quillen, Zach, 53, 57, 59–60, 65

race, 78–80, 91
rap, 9, 12, 19, 21, 22, 30, 32, 70, 79–80, 91
Reid, L. A., 62–63

"Same Love," 59–60, 61, 66, 70, 74, 76, 80
   Grammy performance, 87–88
Schott, Julie (mother of Ben Haggerty), 18
Seattle, 10, 17, 18, 31, 35, 38, 40, 44, 49, 53, 74, 91, 95
Shark Face Gang, 58
Snoop Dogg, 30
Sony, 58, 62–63
Spokane, 25, 28, 31

technology, 32
30/30 Project, 28, 29

"Thrift Shop," 10, 31, 61–62, 65, 66, 69, 80–81, 91, 92
   Grammy Nomination performance, 7–11
"Town, The," 44
Tupac, 20, 21, 30

Unplanned Mixtape, The, 44
Urban, Keith, 12

"Vipassana," 20
VS, 48, 50
VS. Redux, 48

Wansley, Michael "Wanz," 10–11, 53, 77
Warner Brothers, 65, 66
"Welcome to Myspace," 37
"Welcome to the Culture," 22–23
"Wing$," 59, 70–73
Wu-Tang Clan, 21, 31

You Can Play, 88

ABOUT THE AUTHOR

Judy Dodge Cummings is a writer and history teacher who lives in south-central Wisconsin. As a kid she liked to write poems and as an adult she likes to read them. A lifelong lover of rock 'n' roll, classical, and pop music, she never figured herself for a hip-hop fan. Writing this book has changed her mind. Rap is musical poetry.